A Sorting of the Ways

New and Selected Poems

also by Ricardo Quinones

North/South: The Great European Divide
(U Toronto P 2016)

Fringes
(39 West Press 2015)

Finishing Touches
(39 West Press 2014)

Roberta and Other Poems
(39 West Press 2011)

Through the Years
(39 West Press 2010)

Erasmus and Voltaire: Why They Still Matter
(U Toronto P 2010)

Dualisms: The Agons of the Modern World
(U Toronto P 2007)

Foundation Sacrifice in Dante's "Commedia"
(Penn State UP 1994)

The Changes of Cain: Violence and the Lost Brother
(Princeton UP 1991)

Mapping Literary Modernism: Time and Development
(Princeton UP 1985)

Dante Alighieri
(Twayne 1979; updated revised edition 1998)

The Renaissance Discovery of Time
(Harvard UP 1972)

A Sorting of the Ways

New and Selected Poems

Ricardo Quinones

39 WEST PRESS
Kansas City, MO
www.39WestPress.com

Copyright © 2011 by Ricardo Quinones

All rights reserved. No part of this book may be reproduced, scanned, or distributed in any printed or electronic form, including information storage and retrieval systems, without permission. Please do not participate in or encourage piracy of copyrighted materials in violation of the author's rights. Please purchase only authorized editions.

First Edition: July 2011

ISBN: 978-0-615-50464-3

Library of Congress Control Number: 2011932739

This book is a work of fiction. Names, characters, places, dates, and incidents are products of the author's imagination, or are used fictitiously, satirically, or as parody. Any resemblance to actual persons, living or dead, business establishments, events, or locales is entirely coincidental.

10 9 8 7 6 5 4 3 2

Design, Layout: j.d.tulloch
Front/Back Cover Horses: Robin Vaccarino

39WP-04A

Many thanks to the very talented Robin Vaccarino for providing the magnificent horses that grace the front and back covers. And great thanks to Jay Martin, Nancy VanDeusen, the late Aino Paasonen (the inspired reader of many of these poems), our NEH gang (Rolena Adorno, Dawn Delbanco, David Michael Hertz), and of course my wife, Roberta L. Johnson.

Contents

Foreword   ix

From *Through the Years*

The first thing out tramping	3
Newspapers	5
Aggressively, Kansas	7
SoCal: A Sorting of the Ways	9
Wallet Poems I (1, 2, 4, 5, 7-10)	12
Why Do Grown Men Weep?	16
Uncles	18
Gilbert Paoli	20
Esau (as spoken by the man himself)	22
Wintertime Sun	24
Wallet Poems II (1, 3, 5-10)	26
Domestic Arrangements	30
Domestic Interrogative	31
Architectura (after the Statue at the Bargello)	32
A Woman Dead	34
Photograph of an Aged Woman Amidst Her Iris	36
Atonements	37
An American Writer	39
Wallet Poems III (1, 2, 4-6, 8)	41
Desert Bloom	46
A Glass of Deep Red Wine	48
Wanderers	50
Oil and Water	52
Final Things	53

From *Roberta and Other Poems*

Odalisque	57
For Roberta on Her Birthday	58
Delight and Reserve	60
February 15: Roberta's Day	62
Rocks and Their Fellow Travelers	64
Wallet Poems IV (1-4)	70
Dispatched	73
Profanities	75

New Poems

The Grafting Tree	81
Ten and More	83
To Pick a Penny	86
Wallet Poems IV (5-10)	89
Wallet Poems V	94
Bloc Notes	96
Spoiler Speech	99
A New Beginning	102
Early and Late: The Hazards of the Ways	106

Foreword

Poets and their first volumes are out on a limb. Poets take their chances, sending out their works to an unknown reception. Their poems, like children, must make their own way out in the world without any letter of certification, barely a work permit. But to add letters of defense reeks of defensiveness.

I, however, would like to add some comments about *Wallet Poems*, mainly because they represent the kind of insights that only occur to practitioners. The qualities and purposes of these poems are on display in *Wallet Poems I.1*, *I.10*, and *II.3*. One day, while reading a small poem, I realized that it had need of companions, of cohorts. Thus emerged the plan to set the *Wallet Poems* apart, to group them in separate listings with numbers to boot. But as they made their merry ways, a change occurred. *Wallet Poems* themselves accredited their own demise. They outgrew themselves, becoming something else instead. (This change over is recorded in *Bloc Notes 1*, the inheritor.) One cannot say that they will be missed, since they will always have their established positions. What will be missed is the joy of their easy fetching. The beggar king is dead; long live the beggar king.

–Ricardo Quinones

FROM *THROUGH THE YEARS*

The first thing out tramping
Is to roust a sleeping stick,
Good for knocking at trees
Or golf about the leaves.
Sight down a shot or two,
Ward off critters and feral things
Club to smithereens.
One that comes ready to hand,
Doughty and bluff at the end,
Tapered smooth at the grip,
A natural extension of self,
And a pendant part of striding,
Like crunching deep in crusted snow.

Newspapers

Why do we read the papers,
A world in which we are only part at home?
A ritual of reconnection
After night's salt sailings,
A national debriefing time
Of stewing at the village well
Or grousing at the kitchen table.
A daily diet of madness
Of verification and some acclaim
Or is it simply a short attention span
The solidarity of the commonplace.
Where nothing strays,
Yet everything stays—like the evening news—
At a level of depression,
Like radon on the cellar stairs.

It's a glaring register of fact
—Yes, that describes what did happen,
That was you with the digits of age—
Undeniable and inadmissible
Mug-shots taken on trust.
One-by-one they stand there
Line items with no veto.
Yet facts unstoried can't possibly add up.
For this we take to dreams,
Or Shakespeare's last plays.
They bring back tales and fearing times,
Wrongings real and true,
Fittings that we hazard to recall.

That's why we read the papers.
It's a gathering time,
A way of filling up
The useless and the random,
Collectibles to no purpose,
Horrors to no event.

They all must go someplace,
If only to dream's seven doors
With only one bullet in the gun
Yet these doors are corridors that meet
Tunneling and furnishings found
You only need to plunge down one
—that's all the steps it takes—
To plunder room and begetting room.

Aggressively, Kansas

Who's on call for Kansas
With its subtleties of sunken rage?
Where in the men's locker room
Signs in hand-written scrawl
Chasten the brazen and the bold
"Others are tired of your parts
Hanging out all over."
Modesty cloths spread over sprawl.
Concealments that bring to the fore.

> Frost is on the window, drift is on the pane
> Frost will go and come again
> Write with the finger, write with the pen
> Frost will run and come again

Picket fences are guardian rails
Masterpieces of daggered inflection
Swords pointed up, blood humiliation
Containing sledge that won't recede
All sufficiencies of evil within

> Frost is on the window, drift is on the pane
> Frost will go and come again
> Write with the finger, write with the pen
> Frost will go and come as rain.

Like God's lightning it shivered the earth
And instantly severed the chord.
Oh unminding twittering squirrel
Caught in an effigy of prayer
—Oh hart that pants—
A red-tail hawk squandered your last meal.
With talons like manacles it straddled its prey,
Between the Union and Strong Hall,
The lunch-time crowd cordoned itself,
Confounded by that great event.

Who could dislodge him from his rightful seat,
That broad forehead and rigid stare,
The natural instinct of grand design,
Flocked in self-determining fate,
Pinioning its primal erotic mate.
It plunges its beak but to withdraw
Like dangling pasta the smoking entrails.

> Frost is on the window, drift is on the pane
> Frost will go and come again.
> Write with the finger, write with the pen,
> Frost will run and come again

So pick it up bleeding Kansas,
Where no one catches a word on the wing,
Baffled by any thrown-out fling.
Work that line of words at risk,
Like a bullfighter all sheen and piffled color,
Whose body is bent like a fiddler's bow
At the mound of groined exposure,
Each time, each sand, each roar
Taking the chance of contact direct
The sacerdotal function of respect.

> Frost is on the window, frost is in the grain.

SoCal: A Sorting of the Ways

"All people are the same,"
Breezing she goes over her bubbly,
"Oh no they're not,"
Passing on the fly I let out,
With which I am glad to say
Even my masseuse agreed
Though she doubled down on diversity

Thus began my recent run
Of California skirmish
My adopted native land
Once again my chest hollow sinks
At the latest gush of fabled wealth
Flotillas of pricey models
Preen as they parade
Through every street and strip
Barracuda-eyed and snub-nosed
Contoured additions to the terrain

Down that sink-hole cycle
I did not need the vocal brand
"STK PRFT"
On a Bemmer tooling by
"I am glad you spent it dear," I think
"But need you advertize the haul?
Wasn't older wealth more discreet?
They didn't shower in the street."
Democratic ease and sufficient opulence
Was how Whitman wanted it
And particularly better
If the getter knew how it was gotten
Or was somewhat philanthropic.

My heart jumped
When barely an hour later
An apparition rounded the verge
Of my condo complex road
A retired couple—no down-and-outers they—
She quite pert in her synthetic whites
And he slim trim and neatly tucked
Carrying a pick-spade in one
And in the other hand a veggie bag
Something had clearly turned round
The tunings of southern Orange County.

You can bet my converse was eager
Magi never met an equal joy
A communal garden they were tending
And he rattled off the shades of lettuce
Iceberg, romaine, escarole and more
Like Bottom I was delirious
With sweet peas and snap peas
Keep ringing them up, please, I implored
20 x 20 plots of land-fill
With water twenty dollars a year,
I thought we were back with FDR
Pilfering was of no account
They had a renewable resource
And didn't need what they didn't have.

Such sorting of the ways:
Diagonal from these municipal plots
Students zoom up in sporty cars
And uncontrollable apparel
Parents wait their wagons throbbing
Yet symphonists still master on
With brows of concentrated fervor.

        My own way stepped far back then
        To our own "Victory" garden
        When through hot summers of WWII
        Over the Lehigh River bridge
        I carried our baskets of produce
        Hoards for winter storage
        Festive salads on our Italian table
        Those medleys of color and chord.

That very eve of the big Spring change
The crescent first moon
Hung phosphorescent and alone
Except for Venus
Minding the ladle
As my friend Rik explained
Whose growth on his prostate
Is to be cut come Monday prime.

Wallet Poems I

1.
Wallet poems you carry with you,
All folded up with proper care,
Like sheets in the hallway closet,
Like books perched high on a chair.

Like sheets their use is private,
Like books they're read alone.
Release them their confinements,
Distend their wings in air.
Like sheets, like books, you'll find
Matters sufficient for play—
The common places of the everyday.

2.
Don't be harsh, my dear wife
Against those circling rings.
Love handles are gifts of age
And the fruits of a happy life.

Like trees they only add to core
The bark where I take hold,
When in our striving love
You come to ask for more.

4.
I hate the extensions of winter,
Thirty days run on of thirty below.
They're like irrationalities of sound,
A bellowing mutt, a slamming door
Or temblors that won't die down.

There's something willful in extension,
That dogged persistence of prolong,
The same thing on and on.

Less is more where infinity's the scope,
Something arguing a quietness of style.
Isn't once and done good enough?
Why pull from the bag
All that bric-a-brac stuff,
Down to each everlasting chug?
Infinity is undone by an addition of one.
Infinity is always the same.
But one is a nonesuch,
And that is unique
And everlasting just as much.

5.
Pillow talk will land us all in jail,
Those amorphic utterances of grunt and twist,
Argotic grimaces of vengeful thrust,
No need for words where gestures suffice.

The genius of love absolves us there
Turning the gleam of aggressive intent
To stilled thoughts, quiet and touching care
And thus declares us innocent by event.

7.
How could she possibly be a lover,
Who tends those scars of slighted merit?

It's wrong to love another more than self,
Why love that which loves not you?
Unreturned calls that don't measure up,
Deliberations of avoidance clear,
From people you'll find not of your sphere.

But that sadly will not matter
When image of the mind takes hold,
The need to quell that which wants not you,
An imperial instinct to control
That converts to prey hunter and bold.

Love cannot be more nor less than self
But rather seeks that which has no end,
Magnetic drawings of tumultuous embrace,
Those things that bring us face to face.

8.
We don't choose the day, the day chooses us.
Like quarterbacks returned from long time out.
Who is to know why things didn't mesh,
An unreckoned lurch, baggage all spilling.
Poor teaming, poor timing, certainly not merit?
Head and heart geared to purposes diverse.

And now in age the truth comes back,
Beyond deserts an in-pouring,
Ease of place offers such squaring,
One not unrelated to merit.
He paid hard for acquisitions of the way,
The accumulated graces, the exactions of delay.

9.
A large couch is heaven's treasure
Supporting the ways we work,
Flat-out, reclined, or legs akimbo
It does not matter as to worth.

Capacious in the TV room
Where three can sit per view,
It's best used as a love-boat,
Where I first toppled you.

10.
A poem may be like poke,
All rectangular and bulk,
Until it sets to jostling,
Like child in womb
All bend and flurry
Of arms and angles

Messing to take place,
Bringing to force
Recognitions that stagger
Revelations, a face.

Why Do Grown Men Weep?

Why are grown men weepers?
Not late-hour TV hucksters.
But Camus, Naipal and surely others,
Caustic, who write standing up.

It has something to do with fathers,
Now long gone but signaling wrongs.
A single concavity of space
That's present like an amputation.
Definitely a man's thing,
Not like women who flood on occasion,
These weep on no occasion at all.
You might as well bawl at open air
Or decades of emptiness consumed.
Ampler meanings are required here.

With Freud some dark event intruded
When sons throttled the expiring King.
Far gone and muddled for our story
Its implications still are grave,
Pointing to prevailing conditions:
These natures non-communicative
Awkward to urinate side-by-side,
The clogged strengths of muffled truths
And inner beasts they daren't surrender.

There's still offense and injury keen.
Think of Samuel Johnson bare-headed
Absorbing the penitential rain
All day where he did his father wrong.
But such contrition is extreme
A glowing gift earned by few.
Baroque repentance may be forgone
If this one thing is kept in mind:
Tit-for-tat will care for that.

Compensation calls for equal shares
What sons did fathers in turn is theirs.

These considerations may be tabled.
They are things done, incidents of scale.
We are calling up things that never were,
Contrary to event or what was inferred.
That's why grown men weep,
Watchmen of their fathers inert,
It's from pictures in the mind
Missed conviviality of accord,
Something never to be given,
Something stayed as men with kind
Not past times to reopen
But times not given to return.

Fathers' gifts are sleights-of-hand.
What's not there counts the most.
We picture them with arms of bounty,
Hams and sacks and bottled things,
Or perched for dust at a cowboy movie
Or circled with chums at the shore,
And we join in with voice elated
"Isn't this the cat's own balls!"
And they all hulking nod for sure.

We can never be truly convivial.
One perishes by the other's gain,
All those shiftings of generational weight
Are staffings out by the trail.
Perhaps some meeting at Resurrection gate,
But that's past ours to paint
And that's why tears assail grown men.
They understand how all things end.
Never to be righted, and beyond recall.

Uncles

The luckiest thing for a little girl
Is to have gigantic uncles
Such as guard the approaches
Not letting any cut-throats in
Nor handy-dandy hooligans
Let alone some fairy prince.

Boxes they bring of brightened desire
With secret drawers and brassy knobs
Beads and brooches they contain
All spilling like sparkles of fire.

They pitch and throw her about
In widening circles of willing dare
Circus performers of beaten skill
Never held such certain hands
Or felt their swings so secure.

Later they will tender her first drink
A martini mixed with swirl
Held up to the light and sipped
To the delight of any lady-like girl.

Watcher wardens of the place
Designers of adventure free
Just think what our world would be
Without such hands to sculpt our space.

Yet, come as come it must, cancer,
The physics of other inscrutable ills.
But that does not diminish what's begun
Guardians now mounted on walls
Still residents of the place
Claiming new generations
Substances that cohere

Stabilities of choice
With speech that does not err
An openness to engage
Without a flicker of fear.

Gilbert Paoli*

We should all be made into bronze
And cast as Olympian superb
Models of healthy aspire
Fronting the Institut Pasteur.

But in bronze there is no quick,
That paper-weight of imposing mass
No saving breath or sweat in pores
Wearing a walkman of containment
A blinding to whatever occurs.

Quick is what we had
In LA after the War
Crescendo, Ciro's, LaRue,
That was before '72,
When the hippies came to sit
And occupied the Strip.

No master's hand, no grand design,
Inadvertence unschooled
Conveyed its own gathering art
Beyond our skills to contrive,
Moments too happy to know
Because you were the moment,
And by its own inverted light
The moment was you.

Not a series of moments,
Rather a texture of commotion,
Call it an epoch, a swirl,
Or simply a snag in the line.
The only art they could own
Was that of marvelous display.
But this much we can secure,
They had their world in their time,
With no sense of being passed by.

Like a long happy, lucky love
Never a thought as to end,
But simple vibrations to a feel,
Except for some mindfulness
Exalted by a judgment fit
Calling to all who'd listen,
"Never such times again."

And just as certainly
As market's overnight plunge
It was gone from sight
A strange relinquishment
As of a borrowed thing,
Or an old adhesive's rip
That preciousness in time
Not to be found in art
Only the bending circles of smoke
And receding ash that old men stoke.

Gilbert Paoli was a prominent restaurateur in the period described; he was also the model for Health outside the Institut Pasteur in Paris.

Esau
(as spoken by the man himself)

Heavy-lifting is the hard-hat part
Then comes some alec with a tart remark
Like dropping in for the kill
On a cross-word puzzle
With only a few blanks to fill
Or some brigand
Vaulting debonaire
Breathes over your solitaire
And then strides off
Like Charles Darwin
Or Achilles over the asphodel.

Then I go wild
Against God's scales
It's like someone getting mad
At you for getting mad
But I was there first I wish to state
That was my land
Don't I have my rights
The pioneer, the first comer
Not these prodigal Johnnies
Waltzing through the daffadowndillies
At some cherry-picker's ball

Get smart is turnabout
Here all is for the play
Now by device I leave some spaces
And watch them bloat
To plunk down the pimp
Or, fatting them with puzzle pieces
I smile to watch them jump the fit
That's jollifying those tadpoles
Just ducky that vie en rose
It's called keeping on your toes.

Now I get the meaning of sin
Mocking God's plan
Chuckling over small triumphs
It's a withering within.
Wear a fish-hook with happy style
Return smile for plastered smile
With a better hand
Fold before the bettings started
Warrant a petty insight piercing smart
Knowing it's far off the mark
With scissor-kicks of injured merit
I play out the trickster's part
Not joying in another's delight
But trading score-cards of despite

Wintertime Sun

I have a romance
With the wintertime sun
I scuttle indoor plans
To sit all hunched in its glaze
My covered pate cranes
Like seagulls lining the shore
All driven to front the glow.
It doesn't beat down from above
With blinding garish blaze
Where you have to raise your hand
To fend off the glare,
But forehead to forehead straight
Translucent like pearly light
Behind a silken screen
Expends its brightness everywhere.

So different from everything
Of which it is a part
It's an earnest light
A willingness that's ingrained
An economy of appeal
Like words that hold to their mold
On their purposes intent
And won't let go
Blotting out all intrusions—
Blithering TV commercials,
Radio traffic reports
Repetitions without end
The Dionysian Hollywood stars
And their celebrity touts—
Dead before they even begin
Thus laboring to perish from within.

I'll take this time, this season
With all its shortness of hours
O wintertime sun
You've saved the best for last

Wallet Poems II

1. "Strippins"
I met an old enemy
Now defunct of mind
It's hard to find advantage
In such catastrophes of kind
Encasements
Like when we were kids
Fishing at the "strippins"
With twig and pin and twine
Waters black and cold
When all the takings have been mined

3.
Wallet poems are light in purse
Like bills
Mere tokens in verse
Of the bigger stuff around
Like assets banking otherwheres.
They are just the gleanings
The interest earned
Grabbings that abound.
Neither ejected members
Nor bills of state
But happy little wanderings
Sleepers doting on the sly
Without extra weight
Good to fill a pinch or two
And in that way carry their freight.

5.
His mind has taken to hiding.
He has given up trying to decipher
Its cramped and ragged writing
Like a heart beat flattened out

Like the kids gone to Florida
Where nobody's seen again.

By practiced notes to himself
And other furtive ruses
He labors to rehearse what it was
He thought he knew
Like a child wobbling to walk—
Before relinquishing the tangle
And putting down where it says he is.

**6. Geastich li l'olam (I entwine you forever)
    from an Hebrew wedding prayer**
My head in your crotch,
Yours in mine ensconced
Thus all sleep enpretzelled
Topsy-turvy, toes upcurled
Like children, like twins in womb
Not forbidden
But by Good Words enjoined,
"One body, one flesh"
Add to them "one mind"
And they might show how married love
Is fully entwined.

7.
Your hair all flaxen and afly
Your cheeks burnished as autumn
Your smile running to broad as the moon.
You did not know love was such a harvester

8.
Don't blame tautology.
That legacy of botched survey
Is a roundabout along the way
Making unsure direction's flow
Alternating either way "get" with "go."

There's a substance that precedes knowing
What's to do gets done by going
We can grasp the map's markers
Only after marching's started
Dust in the eyes makes vision smarter.

This hitch so orders our things
We only make love when love is in us
We only make do when already so-so
Waltzing conveys the steps of the dance—
Knowing is not an incoming beam—
But what comes from our projecting screen.—
A circle is not that vicious
Just making sure we touch all the bases
—a purpose that governs—
Bringing "home" before "run"
Making us end where we've begun.

9.
I called out "Go to Hell"
To my Parkinson's last night
—Stalking the table
Running shot after shot —
Mingled with other abuse,
"You miserable fake, you."

But it just stood waiting
A bit stepped back
Chalking its cue—
Expecting my next mistake

10.
The most libidinous thing
(By me most certainly drawn out)
Is to hear my wife tell
Of her past lovers and love.

Sizes, I'm afraid
Attentiveness for sure
Ineptitudes of a few
Some dangerous rendez-vous.

Her compliance is reluctant
Only to set the record straight
While I
Operate under constraint
As if it were my immediate stake.

O happy, happy love
What arrows you throw
Not only bolts of pictured fire
But other tinglings there
—As bow takes to quiver—
All conspiracies of desire.

Domestic Arrangements

Lines drawn in the sand
Are meekly futile, largely offensive
Like pre-marital agreements
Divorced from the start
Legalized principles of discord
Invitations to infringement
The "mine" and "thine" of mediated blight
Like fridges with halves consigned,
Like markets readied for flight.

Something abject here took hold
Mechanical rules of the house
Boundaries turned outside in
Guns trained on their own,
What really should be a DMZ
A duty-free zone of intent,

Where we wander as we might
Like crossing the street
At a scramble corner
Without need of light
Telling us when to go, to stop,
Or keep to the right.
Such things are needed
But not by regulation.
They come down from love
Unmuddled by calculation.
Married love has more to mean
Than merely rules of self-regard
Its great task is just to be
Eager expectation
And first morning's sight
Not turned away, squiney-eyed
By severe applications of right.

Domestic Interrogative

As an instrument of blunt force
A question is a remark.
It might not shut any door
In a momentous, final manner,
Nor seem a summons to the witness stand
Like being called to give a reason.
It's a domestic interrogative,
As, "Did you do the thing you went to do?"

The point-blank question direct
Is hardly aggressive, maybe captious
That's not what puts us out,
It's the normal insulating effect,
As if it were ours alone to perform
And not that of the questioner.
The burden all pushed to one side,
Not that from which the pushing comes.
As if only one were to be remitted
While the fulcrum of the world
Sends its gore point to the other.

It does scare up enormous shifts
Packing us off to other inquisitions,
Did it have to come to point direct,
Could not more have been said,
"Was it a successful trip, my dear?"
Or, "I hope the wait wasn't too long?"
More like an out-stretched arm,
Beholding a structure of design,
Circumambient and refined,
Not the stiff shoulder shove
That frisks away the figment of love.

Architectura
(after the Statue at the Bargello)

Isn't it odd
That architectura is a woman
When the bestrident male
Might better intend the epitome's mold
Like the bronzes of Riace
At which women have been known to weep
To see in living form
Their dreams of young athletic grace
And leaping spirits not pinned by weight.

Back on earth their arms athwart
Show a readiness of response
Equal to any situation
Even their ribbed torsos
Like jutting palazzo walls
Or a bulldog in tow
Clearly bring to mind
The Mart of jowly Chicago
Or the squat rotary phone
Now happily replaced by the roam.

Hard to ignore the tall ones
That set all the cities vying
Those stretched sky-walks
Wonders of man-child's intent
Not very subtle in their aspiring
Burrowing upwards to the firmament.

Such agitation is not woman's thing
Imagine suffering The Ring.
No, no! That Architectura is feminine
Has to do with a dignity of holding
An arm that beckons
In refined enfolding
Alignments of embrace
A tendency to assuage
Solicitations of care
Mitigations of malaise
Giving us to know our belonging there.

But the billowing adumbrations
Her draping folds of stony dress
Impart other directions as well.
Like Ariadne's string of clues
They are weavings to no clearing
They landscape a journey
Of mountain passes
Throwing some wrinkle in time
Part Circe's mischief
Part Penelope's rule.
All they require is a willingness to sustain
With no turning back after the first foot-fall.

These circlings round of arm and gown
Are openings that astound
Containments of space
That bring to hatch the warmth of the sun
And yes
Apollo fronting the lineaments of the race.

A Woman Dead*

I hardly knew what it meant
When I heard she was dead.
Nor did the Episcopal service help
Meager in its needy celebration.
Better a cadenza, a fandango
Feet stomping, glasses broken
Even a flat Western drawl,
"She's stiff as nail in a wall."

Three more famous deaths
Left her in their paper traces;
First, Longdon, that winner of races
Now surpassed by Shoe, Pinky and Baze;
Then Vietnam's pot-shot artist
Who strangely bore Walt Whitman's name;
Then Kid Gavilan, my boyhood champ,
Showy with his bolo extravaganza
Ended shining shoes in Castro's Havana

But these are only buttons of fame
The crust but not the bread
She was not made of that stuff
Oh the movements of this friend
Her walk was so fluid
You swore her knees did not bend.

Only rage disfigured her motion
That of women abandoned by mates.
Begun by her father, of course,
Who decamped when she was budding
Not helped by a mother who hates.

No wonder her line was war,
The Gestalt of, but war all the same,
And dropped her Southern double name
Or occasionally fell for the allure
Of a younger woman's flair.

She never engendered
No robin red breast popping seed
But neither did she bear indifference—
Letters not answered, calls not returned—
Her responses were immediate
And broke from the ends of her veins.

And so one made room
Allowing that fluidity of motion
To come to a flowering of grace
Another bright whisk in the particularities of place.

Johnny Longdon was a jockey who had won more races than anyone in his time. When asked if that meant he was the best, he replied, "No, but one of the best." Walt Whitman Rostow was advisor to Presidents Kennedy and Johnson; he was notorious for coming up with one-hundred plans, ninety-nine of which were terrible. Kid Gavilan was a talented fighter with a flashy style, such as the bolo punch.

Photograph of an Aged Woman Amidst Her Iris

Nature grants no respite;
In its dispatches
Holding back is not the way
High embarrassments are thus engendered
Like pudenda laying bare
Or all those swords strapping there
Those things not to be shunned
By an aged woman amidst her iris
Whose growths overtop her quite.

Still she holds to all that splay
The grit that photos convey
Her head slightly weighted
Weavings down from her thinning hair
Forming an oval of studied suggestion
On her breasts own sagging combine
A darkening that's sure to smite
An end in sight
A mandala of hooded grief
An amulet of offered speech
Hands enclosed in a tableau of prayer
Coupling a dome of thatched embrace
All that Mary—virgin and mother—
Was brought to bring
A knowing that's biological and spare.

Atonements

The hero drags a punishing sack
An extremity of grace to atone
Just enough to blunder his step
Or alter his pace to stuttering effect.

Great storage is its own betraying
A club foot, a lump on the back
Those partners in pain
Burdens necessary to assume
Misdirected, distracted, untamed.

That is why he's many years gone
The penalty is actually an urging
A forced uprising that extends the run
A necessary span to permit an unfolding.

    Odysseus doubled his time
    For barking his name
    Dante an equal amount
    For pulling the Pope's tail
    And Shakespeare, mighty Shakespeare
    (Wagner is beyond repair)
    More sinned against than sinning
    But sinning nonetheless
    How else explain such injured exclaim
    Before relenting he forgave.

But it is not the extent of space
Nor the travel of years that matters
They're only numbers that shadow
The shouldering burden he carries.
Before what he knew as possible only
He now hails home by bone and damaged bearing.

Driven by a strange excess
To arrive at his just intent
Those declarations he intended to make
Now come unbidden
With nothing else to attend
Fronting the force of the winds
And down the accumulated years

The American Writer

Not all return from battle
Not all imbalance is restored.
Hemingway comes to mind, our native son,
All shoulder, strap and sword
A first-rate man acting as third,
Straddling legs, and arms extended,
A barreling master of bar-room brawl,
Of combat patrols and wars he won.
How could that man consent to lie,
Repeal at source language he crafted
And the stern truths he tended?

Don't blame that man for lordly claims
Even stupidities of vile demeanor.
His wounds went back too far,
Parcels detained, garments derided,
Abusings that came to stay
Like a field of error acquiring mass
Determining a line of raucous behavior.
Perhaps he no longer wished to give of his time,
He who already had given so much.
Straitened so between two lives,
Observed and always observing.

Make no mistake there was consentment,
A frontier audaciously breached,
Like owing oneself another drink,
Or straying into a punishing car,
Steel shoved to the head of the mouth.
There is in death a skilled inclining,
A willful phantom of abandon,
That we can know but not determine,
The sudden freedom of letting go.

Now we can know those figures he mounted.
That long-lunging, harrowing regale
Whose gleam he trafficked downwards,
Throwing back time eventful and free,
Claiming his place with splendid cast,
No stumbling slippage or wincing shame,
Where no shark comes to strip his gain.
Just Ernest, Cal Lowell and their originals in crime
The Kid named Billy, other mountebanks sublime.
No scraps for salvage from death's passing trains.
A teeming wildness breaks from their veins

Children of Luck they lived to wager
Chancing a grandeur of living fame
Now at this moment of final time
Let it pour down like cleansing rain

Wallet Poems III

1.
Scooting along the airport concourse
In a tightly-fitted cart
It's not wrong to give thumbs-up
To those who trundle along
Even those who pass on walk-ways
To slightly quicken their pace.

It's like rolling down a diamond lane
With open country in sight
Past the braking singles
The only things to balk the flow
Are looky-lous who go too slow
Or cars not keeping to the right.

Such exalted riding
Should offer no offense
To gods—or other-worldly beings—
It's so small a recompense
For all the vengeful bolts
That struck my buoyant striding.

2.
"Love ensued
Followed by marriage
Followed by children."

Such matters, irreversibly stated
Are too much in a line,
Like pictures in a family album
They follow from a start.
Why not the reverse?
I've seen children
Followed by marriage
With love bailing from behind.

We cannot return omelet to the egg
Or start a scaffold from the top
Even back-tracking a home run
While it flies in cricket
Is in baseball clearly out
Bringing all things to a stop
But change of course in living
Argues an effort of trust
What works one way
The other can bestow as much

Callings are not bases
To be touched in order given
Or numbers in serial pursuit
But buildings-up of fullness
With abundance sought en route.

4.
Obits have acquired some style
They're much in view and amply read
Occupying more than half a page
With gleaming photos riding high
They seem to wave as you go by
And kill you with a smile.

Even by-lines are provided
Like signatures on works of art
Nothing is left outside
Not even cause of death
—from once we used to smart—
Although some, like pancreatic cancer
Still bring occasion for fear.
For AIDS there's always partners
Or complications left untold
While divorced mates are placed on hold.

Nothing like it used to be
With dank columns all in a row

One on top of other
Like cemeteries in Spain
Intercalations of corpses
Families all together run
Even the borders dressed in black
They hewed to the basics
Not things we were anxious to learn
They called it propriety
The stance of things held private
Not meant for public show.

5. "Festina Lente"
Married love moves slowly by delay
It sheds garments one by one
—no rampageous clumpings on the floor
Nor cries of havoc like declaring war—
And puts away all in detail
Or hangs neatly to keep the press.
It brushes teeth and removes eyes
And might replace a toilet roll
That casual sense of innings to spare—
Those things in store.
Then proceeds to always find more
Of the gestures of love—
Perpetually the same—
That perpetually restore.

(I do wish she would move it, though)

6. Silence
Silence is not a non-event.
It's not even remote
Most likely it's resolute
Hemispheric and snug
Like an old blanket
Up-close with a touch of fuzz
—Satin is much too sheen—
A containment that's domed
Permeating all.

It's a presence to be known
Even carrying weight
Something we can step through
Like stalking rooms
After a quake
Or cleaving mortuary gloom.

Even when there's noise
Silence can still be heard
Choppers don't matter much
Nor the blowers I thought were banned.
Some dominance of the larger sphere
Beamings in the air
And sendings down
That only ask our waiting.
Like solitude
It follows the promptings of mind.
Hence all those pourings of sound.

8.
There is a song
I hear the Cubans sing
How the flowers weep
And other such inordinate things

To hear Omara's song
You know the streets she's roamed
And even Ibrahim comes along
To count his woes and ways
But I want to say
Adding a bit to their trouble
You don't need the flowers
I can contribute to the treble
Believe me my baggage is full
—My cause is great—
I glisten too
As much as the flowers would do.

Even as I limp along
I harbor those tears;
They are, as I now know,
The springs and source of song.

Desert Bloom

It's springtime in the desert
And the people throng
To watch the flowers flourish
A scrum of colors
A palette of hues
Even indigo, a blue beyond the blues
A splurge of hope and recovery
They take no mind of brevity—
The billowing colors' splash
Destined under the pounding sun
To return to its original ash
Gone until next year's return
The immensity of the desert's sands
Once held in the depths of the sea.

Like the Easter Saturday vigil
Expecting some rebirth
The congregations gather
In their defiant colors
Are bid to hold hands
And embrace across the pews
The priestly figures intercede
They look so distantly small
Choreographed in an ancient mural
Like miniatures in a play
Diminished by the ascending church walls
They bravely elevate the hosts
And daintily dab the goblets' lips

This is my body
This is my blood
Do this in remembrance

After 54 years I resume my station
And melt the dried wafer
In the heart's springtime
Ready to make my response
The answer called out of me
Remembrance
That is how I finally get it
Jesus is our study
A figure of assent
A vessel of memory
Do this…
Remembrance…
An instrument for my dead
The hope that beckons the faith
That one day we shall all come together
And stand where we have always stood
Before the burnt desert sands
And the worlds beneath the seas.

Grant it only twenty per cent of the terrain
At the maximum, thirty
That is not nothing
That is still something
A pittance of our gain
Memory and remorse are not in vain
They return us some resource
Like the desert flowers
And we join hands
Against the magnitude of sands
The never-ending space
In this time we take occasion to embrace.

The doors fly open
The voices take wing
All the choral powers
Defy the brevity of spring
Even the dead, we believe, return to sing.

A Glass of Deep Red Wine

Like a model in form
Of beauty beheld
A silken sleeved arm
Lifts a glass of deep red wine
Twirling by the light
And by the candle fire
The tumbler like a tower
With all the world in view
Tells all the bouquet
Tells all the flower
Of human desire.

It shines by dimming light
In a mosaic of flame
Against dark wood
On mirrored walls
A glass of deep red wine
Extended to sight
Tells all the taste
Tells all the glow
In human delight.

On each occasion
A glass of deep red wine
Showers the face
With radiance so ruby
It loosens the folds
Of smile and glance
All the human treasure
That throng and dance
To arouse the senses
To the gifts of pleasure.

The sibilant grace
Of a glass of deep red wine
Before the whispering blaze
Moving with measured pace
From glass to tongue
Undulations of taste
Bringing delight and desire
Whose mysteries now told
Turn flesh to living fire.

Wanderers

You cannot renege on all those years
Though unrequited and of mixed account
They come back in meinie folded
Bearing news from within and without.

Might as well push back the sky
Whose saggings inflect our every view
They are not only that which we know
Their promptings inform the ways we go.

Folk of no particular intimacy
Some of scant amiableness
Vulnerabilities must have their day
Like children peddling cookies
Knockings that can't be turned away.

With no force to gather us in
Their cards of varied appeal
Helpless if nobody's home
Or ever will be again.
They scramble to find their places.

       Vincent, raspy and gruff
       Enticing with bits of medieval lore
       Katherine, like her mother,
       Bent halfway to the floor
       John, like Fuzz, a football great
       Of more thoughtful merit
       Than blackboard teachers can claim
       Bob, dwindling down to death,
       Breaking only once to regret
       Loss of his wife's warm breath.

These are only a few
Not the most notable
Still shadowy and sparse
Whose renewal is plight
By pact I never contrived
Vagrant all these years gone
Faring a wanderer's fate
Flittings that never terminate
Only stayed by reasons of heart

Hardly themselves to maintain
They undertake their watchings
Solicitude meant our way
A selflessness so durable
A pathos without stain
Moments of wonder
Like statues in the rain

I'll do my best, I always say
It's not that easy a task
In my hard pallet and darkened hall
I sometimes tarry the call.

These beckoning apparitions
Come not tuckered,
No blood to siphon away
Or jostle at the freshing pit
It is myself they come calling about
Keeping me to a just account
These perishable goods I sustain
Are stories heard and markings sounded
Holding me to my stash and say.

Oil and Water

Master of the amber marshes,
The brown pelican, emblem of his habitat,
Drives through the wedges of the waves
Larking with the spume of sprays.
Once endangered but returned in numbers
A new strangeness cranks his toil
He is perplexed by the heavy hand
Tightly squeezing his wings
The sludge that weighs him down.
Where is the force of his former lift?
Grace actions have become obstacles
Now he staggers out of the water
And finds relief in hugging the ground.
His head dangles of a piece
Giving direction to where he falls
To rise and pierce the light no more.

Oil and water are our elements
The water that cleanses
The chrism that relumes
Oil and water extend our wings
When at baptism we are relieved
Of the soot that brought us hither
And the clothes we don
Render the soul's picture of white.
Of course this emblem cannot last
Even Jesus above the altar
Has wings distended but cannot fly
So heavy are the spikes
That drill him to the tree
Still his arms are opened wide
Ready to receive us when we too
Return to earth all darkened and stiff.

Final Things

I want to go back again
When my Daddy was my Daddy
And no harm would come his way
Because I was standing by his side.

I want to go back again
When my Daddy was my Daddy
And with weapons of sharpened skill
I stood by his side.

I want to go back again
When my Daddy was my Daddy
And resting in a small bed
I sat by his side.

I want to go back again
When my Daddy was my Daddy
And lowered into the soft earth
I stood sentry by his side.

From *Roberta and Other Poems*

Odalisque

A man might be transformed
But a woman is transfigured
By the gracious beauties of love's intent.
When spread to its full extent
Her body is like majesty unfurled
Her composure is so confidently contained
That beyond her figure there is no world.
She is gifted to the heights of splendor
There is nothing she does not own
Even birds hover in flight
Unwilling to relinquish their place in the light.
Her breath emanates through her pores
Not a particle is ignored;
Her hair when fanned is strewn like willows
And when she stretches
It's as if the world set sail
A picture of grace in a field of motion.
Pleasure abounds at each recommencement
Making it more like a constant flow
An equipoise of undiluted bliss
A sheen of gossamer covers her glow
A Greenwich of time is centered here
From which all things start and go.

From the beginning this was the world's way
Despite what other books might say
A modulated pace of sheer delight
No womb and tomb or death and Eros
Not even Cleopatra burning bright
But a human measure that embodies life
Giving a grounding to the paths of light.
First founded in woman's delight.

For Roberta on Her Birthday

There is a loving beyond love
That doesn't come from below or above
But keeps a constant human sphere
A staunchness of character
A loyalty that adheres
Which gathering through the years
Was not quite understood when we held hands
And together swore those bands.

The reigns of time, biology and history
Certainly have exacted their tolls.
We too were young and foolish
Pushing blindly with the pedal
When the brake worked just as well
Our miscarriages were blatant
Excused only by our need to know
What was urging us through the snow.

And snow it did and does now
As we watch through the window
The magic of wintertime's sun
Our age has slowed us down
The fierce virility a thing long done
But that does not mean we are gliding
Resoluteness of character
And loyalty through distress
Are not passive virtues and have no rest,
Constantly put to the test
By the Nietzschean Uber-mensch
Or the will to power
We know what wisdom has taught
Ours are the lessons experience has wrought
That down through years deliver the trust
The metals that will not rust
A rightness of kind worked by benevolence of mind.

And as we enter the fog of the night
Not much shall remain
Our hands shall crumble
Flat stones shall plane our earth
Our names inscribed thereon
And other fruitless data of years
But not the realities that they meant
Of two people joined by their trusting intent.

Delight and Reserve

Innocence is delightful
But Delight in all its movings
Has an innocence as well.
Delight is totally engaged
And that rarely can go wrong.
Delight that poor man's folly is whole,
Seeking no other support
Nor other minding to bear,
No searchings elsewhere.
Self-sufficing, self-sustained
Attaining in moments direct
An ascendancy not had by power:
We delight in another's delight.
Why priests and gods can do no other
But bless a woman in throes of pleasure.

There is in Reserve an earnest
Not meant for display.
Must all the push be red on black
Florid beyond measure,
With nothing held back
Arms flaying needfully
Over-wrought and beyond contact?
Autumn's colors are fetching, too—
Abundance in Reserve
A mine of memory adhering.
Reserve's still water is private
And its holdings stately,
Correct and never failing speech
Nothing beyond our reach,
Why priests and gods regard as blest
A woman collected, in herself possessed.

They fare different weather
Delight and Reserve, Reserve and Delight
Sisters of bright provenance
Like silver streams from pictured vases
Replenishing our earthly stations
Each making the other better.
Reserve without Delight
Would have no place to go;
Delight without Reserve
Would loosen all in show.

Roberta, my love, they pour in you
Those streamings of lordly treasure
Those beckonings of marital pleasure
If only I can meet them to your measure.

February 15: Roberta's Day*

The pronunciation of your day
Requires no saints to adorn your name.
Come from the Foxes and the Roses
California's bushes and briars
Small farms and horses
That weather your sun-fed ways.

Although no saints abound
This date is honor's stall of renown
More prominent by omen
Of secular saints who work our weal
Impressing as in a seal
Three crowns that meet
To herald your future sway.

It is Susan B. Anthony's day
An abolitionist spurned
Who Christian Temperance turned
Into a Woman's Union
A sisterhood of gentler base
Thus bringing gender to nation and race.

On this date the Maine went under
And capsized too the Empire of Spain
But up there arose the American fleet
And the Spanish generation of '98
Whose cross-fires you came to arbitrate.

Theses two crowns need a third,
But not quite yet.
This date is Lupercalia
Famed for its boisterous feats
When young athletes of bodily sheen
Raced through the narrow Roman streets
Like running of bulls in Spain

Fertility was all the hunt
Not a single string of goatish skein
But with maleness swinging free
Whipping the matrons to a frenzied glee
And a fervor to their stomping feet.

On this date another Anthony
That glorious runner and generous friend
Tempted Caesar with the diadem
Whose leafy coverlet and verge
Provides the august shade
That guards the face
Against those loathsome sprites
Those demons of the sun-lit sky
That pierce and dig more harm
Than all the armies of the night.

So we invoke what birth intended
As signs and figures, forerunners along the way
To be emblazoned on this day.
To the protection of these crowns
We only add this parasol of care
That no harm come to your gentle skin
As you continue to front the winds
And the malevolent powers of the air.

On her father's side, Roberta came from the family of Fox, and on her mother's, from the family of Rose. One of her prominent studies was <u>Gender and Nation in the Spanish Modernist Novel</u>, which was preceded by <u>Crosssfire: Philosophy in the Novel in Spain 1900-1934</u>. She periodically has to be treated for spots of skin cancer, and she was given a parasol on her birthday.

Rocks and Their Fellow Travelers

"Who, moving others are themselves as stone, unmoved ..."
(Quoted by Eva Brann in *Homage to Americans*)

The graven testimony of sense
And the logics of difference
Should make any glossing clear
That nowhere in the catalogues of creation
Does it ever appear
That the Holy Spirit made Rocks and Boulders.
Precious stones, yes, when the rivers parted
But they were only symptoms of decline.

Rocks and such uncreated things
Were there before the beginning
And will still be there after the end.
Nothing like pathetic Gnostics
Who whip up contending Hierarchs
Rocks and boulders forfeit the game
They refuse the play
Indifference is their ready suit.
There is no prestige in the lowest depths
If lower depths fit them all the way.

They come from different worlds
No flourish of trumpets
To announce an approaching King
No generosity of spirit
Benevolence of imagination
Or a compassionate heart
Not even the simple contentment of the Lord
Who surveyed his early work
And found it good.
But drubbed by rocks and boulders
As paltry devices needing to be liked
Or a slavish eagerness to please.

What thy want is just the opposite
Nothing but silence could them appease.

They have no truck even with God's opponents
In whom sentiment has come to uncover
Some tissues for elevation
My Esau about whom a friend wrote
That he was a hard man, a rock.
But he was the victim of a situation
Beguiled and doomed to drudgery
By a younger brother's skullduggery
Never-ending was his moan
About getting back his own.
And weary complaint about patrimony
Which did attract some sympathy
But not from those who live alone
And have no lineage to share
Unmoved and unmoving
Rocks and boulders laugh at what is fair.

Another was Luzbel, the Spanish Satan,
Who fell and fell again
At each relapse his legions grew thinner
Yielding finally to the odds of the winner.
Something boyish even childish
In his aspiration to rule and reign—
No one runs for President seven times
Is the lesson he never learned—
Comic even, like a Jack-in-the-box
But never a buffoon
Some scratch of redemption
In his need to aspire.
As the world goes,
If you add up and compare
The Scriptures are softies
Hardness of heart is mollified and rare.

Pagan classics tell a similar story.

That of Sisyphus
Stuck on the same track
Even the rocks come to deride
And watch him slip and slide
As he approaches the final divide
Believing once again
He will cross the line
Only to stumble
And dodge the rocks that tumble
Down the long mountain side,
Across the shore coming to rest
Wherever they abide
At the bottom of the silent sea.
Wondering what gets into this man
Who rolls his sleeves and girds his tunic
To try again
Only to lose his grip at the final footing.
How could he fail to understand
That after the pinnacle there is nothing to stay
But simply another downhill all the way?
With rocks there is only one outcome
Not even a big splash
No Romantic credit offered for trying
The creaking sound of bone against bone
Is the only sound from stone against stone.

These are fall-guys
Whose dithering brings some esteem;
Then there are those who add to this theme,
Who become like rocks themselves
Closing their lives with a silence so resolute
So far from God but just as absolute.
They deserve their own Rushmore
But rather than facings for all to see
They turn their bodies to the wall
Careless of when the ax lets fall.

Iago is the leader of this brigade

Against the melodrama of Italian rage
With Othello sending up such torments
To crash heaven's battlements
And break loose the falling "stones"
That would mitigate his pain
Or annihilate his brain.
But Iago seeks no such relief
So closed within himself
He knows where to find his end
"From this time forth I never will speak word."
No commendable story does he seek,
Such that would palliate his schemes
Not even death by fire-fed screams
But rather stones around his neck
And casting into the deep,
Where he will assume such a stance
That even the fishes will poke and dart,
Unable to jostle him with a start.

It is only Lear who, as in so much more,
Knows the scandal in its highest sense.
They must have hearts of stone
Who do not howl at Cordelia's death,
Which takes away life's breath
And sends a crack down its middle
Creating a fissure that few can sustain.
Goneril bears her half of the bargain
Their society must endure
This lusting woman who killed her sister.
But cannot be faced down or brought to heel
"Do not ask me what I know,"
Are all the words her scorn intends
Such terseness brings to an end
Any outpourings of remorse,
Or brazen features of a dark renown
Do not lay your speeches on me
What I desire is the stillness at the bottom of the sea
Where no names are known,

No faces shown.

In Dante's infernal lower reaches
There are those who abandoned hope
Long times ago
Virgil trying to pry Bocca's story
Is told that he is out of his league.
Different tickets of transit are required
Not the soft soap of fame
But the hardness of heart
That would banish his name.
Dread silence of blank spaces
No desire, no response
Is adequate to the depths of those sunken faces.

Do you really believe
That Cain slew his brother
With the powdery jawbone of an ass?
Certainly a heavier stone was at hand
Especially the stones enrooted in the hearts of man.
Which for me explains Stonehenge.
They did not lug those ten-ton tocks
To tell the time, or the calendar of seasons
Nor were such ugly things
Suitable monuments to the majesty of kings.
In the roughness of their martial times
They needed twin pillars to express
The double strains in the make of humans.
Overtopping each is the cross-bar
Which serves as cap
Shutting off both desire and response.

God had no need to bring about rocks.
In the hollow chambers of the heart
There was ample space for humankind
To be left to their own concoctions,
Which not even divinity could restrain—
Evidence certain

That rocks and boulders were outside his range—
So free from its taint, he could not invent
The absolute silence of their chilled intent.

Huzzah for the kingdom of stone
And those who no longer aspire
Nor feel any need to atone.
You shall indeed be left alone
Free at last to gnarl your bone.

Wallet Poems IV

1.
TV fans the air waves
With fervent pleas or raves—
"Listen to me" is the constant holler
Like a drunk who has you by the collar—
Leaving a residue of mold
With no pitches left untold
All excited and no place to go
Giving new meanings to "shallow."
The only thing it brings together
Are 5-day plans for the weather.

When what the spirit requires
Is accumulations of thought
Refunding all that is store-bought
Or not self-taught
And brought to hold
Avoiding all that is canned,
Even quelling the tremors of hand.
A treasure hunt of expressive connection
Comes from books of mediated reflection.
Where what is ours puddles around
Until it ready is to be found.

2. A Dirge for Mary
Brimming with sexual pride
She flashed a big rock
"You didn't think I could get a man like that."
A nudge of flaunt we could have done without
But Mary was a novelist, whose heroines
Clawed and battled their ways
Up from the waterfronts of Seattle—
Mary's much-alikes.
Now in her sixties,
Her face cracked and creased

She fell into the sweep of his arms
The smiling bounty of his charms,
This handsome dancing man.
An expert in vibrating toys
And other more parlous ploys.
In months he sapped her savings
And at the last, her beneficiary,
Utilized his laboratory training
To stick with insulin her softer tissue
And take his profits from this woman without issue.

We were later to learn
That the police were on his trail
Waiting for one last kill—our Mary as bait—
Before reeling him in.
Thus Mary, from Seattle's laden docks,
With her own literary skills
Was undone by a male vagrant
Who knew what opened the locks
To woman's long-losing love of love;
Some wild arousal
Almost a taunt
Committed her to places where predators haunt.

3. "Words, words, words"
   - Hamlet

(For Nelson and Stephanie)

Harvey Gross, the prime metricist of his day,
Whose approval expert poets sought,
At heart a composer
Who listened with lights dimmed
So that every note might be caught,
Lay at a hospice in Silver Springs
His body twisted and his mind in shreds
Yet feeling knighted by his book of verse
That Myron Simon and I worked to collect.

Suitably harmonious and precise
This son of the Moderns
Hailed them to every passing nurse.
Or hugged them nightly to his breast
His prosody and pride joined in sleep.
Even when eating he would not let go,
With right hand he gouged slithery pasta
But with his left so guarded his hoard
That not a stain marred their keep.

4.
A poem is drawn to its own completion
Fulfilling a selected pattern of design
But it also has a latent assignment
Working its way through the tunnels of mind.
How else explain its running insistence
And buzzing of a head crying for sleep,
Or phrases bestowed at morning's first light?

Thus Colombo found not the East
But Santo Domingo, waiting to be discovered,
A world that was there all the while,
Ready for its future to come swarming in.

Colombo's was a poetic disclosure;
The moving of each straight and sound
To a purpose they thought they found;
But it was the program they never figured,
That realized itself, unpremeditated, profound.

Dispatched

There, I've done it again
Is it the ingrained habit of the second son
The habit of silence
Withholding of response, or merely delay
That metastasizes into insuperable extent
Where any response is an embarrassment
Impossible to reverse or even repent?

Failure to respond to ally or friend
Even the carelessness of e-mail
Calls for a better explanation
Certainly it is not indifference
A faltering restraint
Nor sluggishness
Where all response is vain,
Nor a wall too high to climb
A simple cartolina, at the ready,
Is all it takes to erase the blame.

Is it a refusal to engage such putty?
Too easy to hasten a reply,
To rally the emotions
To a gregariousness of style?
I've done that often enough
One more time shouldn't be too tough.

Words aren't found wanting
Perhaps it's a sense of bonding
As if the friend were actually there
And didn't need a written record
But knew my reply by affinity's accord.

It's as if we were together in a car
Letting silence prevail
The journey is a long one
There's no need for words
Would the changing landscapes be lost
If we let it all subside?
Are words so important
Most of them redundant
To the binding that presides?

Yes, this is my apology,
A line of defense
Based on the settled nature
That what is will always be
And will not alter
No matter what is said
No packages or letters
Expedited through the air
Will change the meaning of having been there
We sit there forever,
Eternity's heir,
Time is our sediment and not a passing fair.

But some part of me wishes to add
That perhaps a word or two
Would temper the situation
And spare the humiliation
Of having lost our post in what is passing fair.

Profanities

Sitting on the patio deck
Working my then habitual cigar
Watching the zooming cars,
Escapees from the clogged freeways,
Converting streets into speedways,
But not polluting my auditory space
As I think of William Butler Yeats
And the municipal gallery he revisited.
From ballad and tale he knew them all
Those who presided over their times
And showed Ireland's history
In their bark-lined faces.
All coming to life once more in his rhymes.

What would he think of the partners of my youth,
Of Iggy appropriately classed as "ungraded,"
Who came to announce
Where we were fishing for minnies
That George Washington had just died.
This was April of '45;
But he was not far wrong.
For those wrenched by the Depression
As my Aunt Clara would say,
FDR was a savior
To the coal regions of Pennsylvania.

Then there was Ga-ga
Who adopted the stylish mode
Idling his passage along the streets—
Not many cars to hinder his ways—
Straddling a tin-can tied to a string,
Rhythm for the songs he tried to sing.
His brother Chicky was more refined,
As he demonstrated to us kids
How to blow up used rubbers
Through his thick shirt sleeve covers.

Profanities, nothing but profanities
The profanities of the profane.

Or the cowering Gypsy
Knocked clear across the hall
By Mr. Berlin, our principal,
Or his sister, to us kids in awe
Showed how high she could piss
Against St. John's church wall.
And the bug-eyed Jack
Who carried the Gypsy
Across the train tracks,
Where he had been foraging for copper
But found a live-wire instead
His fingers scorched together.
The same Jack who rallied
In Gmoie's favor—
Gmoie of Murder Inc. fame—
And received for his troubles
A State Trooper's club across his brain

Profanities, nothing but profanities
The profanities of the profane.

Or the golden one,
My hero and my star,
Who, as a sixth grader fought ninth-graders—
Can you imagine that? —
And won every game he pitched.
My mother gently came to tell me
That he was killed by the door-handle of a car
Where he was fishing by the canal
Which I still cannot understand
Funerals, o funerals, where we learned to kneel and pray
I bent to kiss his cold hand.

My heroes and my time
The figures go on.

After a winning game in Harrisburg
In which I made some demon shots
Stash conferred recognition
By kissing my head
The same Stash, whom years later,
Meeting disconsolate at a bar,
Told he was "on the bum."
I had no more tears to shed.

Profanities, nothing but profanities,
I would change it all, if I could.
Those things then obscure
Holding poisons without cure,
Profanities without name
We know now what to call them
Profanities of shame.

New Poems

The Grafting Tree

Long years ago
A generous and freshly-married couple
Finishing their first house
Had thought to plant
A sapling oak at the nook
Of their outlying corner lot.
One in time to provide some cover
Of shade for passersby, a respite
Before they trod the rock-ribbed knoll.

In the lines of generation
So popular had this spreading oak become
That latterly some owners thought
A resting place would have purpose, too.
They found amidst some schoolhouse ruins
An abandoned wooden chair
And despite its metal anchorage
Decided to plant it there
So people can sit and rest their feet
A welcomed girding for the knoll.

In time the two became so entwined
The oak's muscular roots
Holding fast the wooden seat
That it became known as the grafting tree,
Fitting so well with the schoolhouse chair.
That people swore they grew together.
No ruffians, thugs or bullies
No matter what weapons employed
Could separate the grafting tree
From the seat it took in care.

The sturdy house still stands
The grafting tree and schoolhouse chair
Still share their place and rooted function
Not much further to explain
Except that natures of a long line
Of energy and repose came together
To overtake even purpose of design.

Ten and More

A normal person can be ten
Three times in a life's span
First there are the children
And Saturday morning soccer spills
Too soon gone, too fast.
One wishes to be ten again
Then predictably grandchildren arrive
With their goals to tend
And muddy leggings to boot
Just as their parents did—not gone at all,
But two in one, revived each Fall.

But the one who squeezes the heart
Was not the last but the first
Oh to be ten again in '45
Joy it was to be alive
To know the thrill
When the church bells began
And one can still remember
At what stone in the pavement
One's foot was raised
As held in a photographic still
Like planted in air
Never to surrender.
Then commenced soldiers' return
And pick-nicks like fairs
Block parties for three weeks
And backyards flowing with beer
Enough to bring closure
To our own wars of Thirty Years.
And the stories anticipated Technicolor
The mementoes, chevrons and lugers
Adding to the home-life treasure.
The kids trying to top each other
Who in conflict would be on their side

Ike or MacArthur
They stretched for the skies
Until finally one luck-minded child
Reaching high trumped all with God
The last choice and best ally
Upon which all forces could rely.

Not too long in the waiting
Came the great revivals.
Baseball, inadequate for the duration,
Regained its play as "majors"
Just as it was in '41
The last memorable season,
Its records still intact.
DiMaggio, Williams and Feller
Back to resume their positions
And New York with three teams packed
Each cheered by men wearing hats.
And boxing, the only other national action,
Received its reigning champ,
Joe Louis, who gave the black man pride,
Before Jackie opened the gates with his slide,
And we all gathered on the front door stoop
To hear epic battles,
Trilogies of sport, Graziano and Zale,
Robinson and LaMotta
When the middle weights were kings
And dominated the rings.

But such times could not linger
Come '52 and '3
I had other stories to learn
I was no longer ten
But pushing seventeen
Now cousins and friends
Were killed or captured
By the Chinese Yalu trap
And MacArthur's blind folly

Now soldiers came home
But by prisoners' exchange
Silent, uncheered by an unsteady nation
Too soon, too fast
The hastening winds of change.

We can never be young again
As we were at war's end.
But nothing can ever suspend,
No arguments however rife
Can ever dim the glisten
Of the moments we shared
When our eyes were only ten
And all things complied
With the glories of those men.

To Pick a Penny

Who would bend to pick a penny
Abandoned like a drunkard
In mystery and misery
On a seedy city street?
Oh penny of debasement
Through what chapped hands
And under what sodden feet
Your once bright mint has passed.
Stores now dispense you free
In order to round out a bill.
Even stuffed with bronze
You are not worth the time
It takes to rack you in the till.

But then, who would not stoop
To pick a penny
About which there is much lore?
No such question would adhere at all
If a sparkling quarter or even a nickel.
Crouched upon the floor.
How could such a wanton coin
Soon out of date
Generate such debate?

In folklore it is a lucky penny,
Or, if you like, the bad penny
That families pay to stay away.
Proverbially, every penny counts
Fortunes begin by adding to amounts
The penny is the firstling of that stock.
In German, who ever scorns a Pfennig
Will never a Taler reap
No one ever called a quarter pretty—
With a penny that's a goodly heap.
But there is more to the penny

Than riches coming your way,
More like a remnant from an ancient world
Its patrimony lies in symbol and myth
Back to days before its coming
Its inheritance was commonly foretold.

Layers of shadows, auras of superstition
Surround the penny.
Putting it straight
Not to pick up the penny
Is a challenge to the gods,
Of hubris the chief offense
As if you can spurn a gift
And your weather will always be fair.
Thus the classical world
Valued kindness to strangers,
Especially beggars in need.
There might be a god behind the stranger
Like Odysseus returning home
Cautiously dressed as a beggar,
A penny of sorts,
Wanting recollection, recall.
One can see a divinity shining bright
In the penny beggar's thrall.
Divinity of those who recompense the right.
The penny is a god-like thing
Reminding all of fortune's fate
That can bring us to a similar estate.

When we bend to pick a penny
We are hitting bottom, too.
That's why I retrieve the penny
It's a kind of forewarning
Of what the gods can send our way.
Handy-dandy who is justice,
As Lear exclaimed, who is thief?
Slippery steps befall us all
From buying houses to living in a car.

We thought we were beyond all that.
A penny was once made of silver
But now sees life as downcast for all,
Heading for the last larger fall.

A tarnished penny, a mere cent
A gateway to the soul, our mustard seed,
Pence of transit to another sight
Where all the pennies are clothed in white.

Wallet Poems IV

5.
("There's not a single verse about the
   poor foot." – from *Out of Africa*)

The French *cinéaste* of subtlety,
Eric Rohmer, drove an entire film
Simply by fixing on a woman's knee.
My fetish would include more couturier.
What sends me are well-tailored slacks
With crease enough to peel a pear
Presiding at a careless draping angle
Over a pair of black high heels
Whose binding straps serve to reveal
The arched expanse of creamy skin
Stretching from toe-hold to cuffs.
The California Club must have been nuts
To ban such attire on female guests
Or they must have been simply blind
Not to be lured by a sight so refined.
As aphrodisiacs go it is more than clear
That women would shop for shoes
Before eating a chocolate éclair.
And I could just sit and stare
Easily the length of a Rohmer film,
Hardly hearing the opera conversation
Except to think, Go and turn your own screw
And the overflights of sexual innuendo.
I have my enchantments here.
With only one leg lifted on the stair
Whatever concoction she would pour
I needed no glass slipper to prevent
It from sloshing to the floor
So eager was my attentive care.
But even wearing the white gloves
That disinfect royal servers

I swear on mounds of holy books
That I could not muster a profane touch,
A greedy violation to be sure
Like scratching oneself during a lecture
I was happy enough to be seated there
In a way transported out of myself;
Adding to the exquisiteness of it all
My lady well knew that I was in her thrall.

6. "Fasten Seat Belt While Seated"
There it rests for all to see
More well-intentioned mundanity
White stitching on a back of blue
It spells at eye-level, unavoidable
But strangely awkward to view.
Not to mention superfluous in sense
Can one fasten a seat belt when standing?
How about floating in the air, or swimming somehow?
Who engineered this feat?
Certainly not the pilot, now "captain" in rank,
With his broadcasting voice,
Or his slushy impenetrable mush
Cadenced in an off-hand manner
Meant to inspire confidence
Like speaking in a trunk,
Or when one was partially drunk.

Could the attendants have lent a hand?
Who sought glamour coaches in the sky
But found their share in waitressing
Laborettes who lost their flair
Pushing heavy carts of food and drink
Up the narrow bumping aisles
Knocking jutting elbows to one side
Except for the uniforms of style
Might as well be in a coal mine.
With its narrow tracks on line.

These pieces of lettered industry
Hand-stitched in sweat shops in Korea
Were bundled by the gross
To be applied in Seattle
Where fittings were none too tight.
Like cover slips a bit time-worn
And clearly outshone by the overhead lights.

These rudimentary stitchings
Clearly command our sight
And while rendering us catatonic
Are not the worst of the blight.
What will they say when we bus to the moon?
Will there be captains, or commanders
Attendants called spacettes
And for once will the sign be right
"Fasten float belts when in flight."

7.
Movies should begin right where they end
Instead of "FIN" they should ask, what then?
After the desolation, crime and death
They enter the long delay of time on hands
From which there is no easy getaway
Try living a life like that.

There is no fast forward, or pause
No previous page, or second take
Or three minutes granted each scene
But a long leash of minutes on end
Weighing like soggy bags of sand.

No grand music to amplify acts
But life as we have it, barren facts
Where we figure how to get along
In the known world to which we belong.

Doldrums are not decompression
Becalmed is not ease of mind
Discrepancies are hard to shake
Bloated are our needs, desperate our take
To match giant images that screens project,
Only drugs can provide the needed fodder
They move the mind to works of wonder
Or better yet, to ease of plunder.

8.
You to whom I opened up
My youthful crazy heart
Dislocated, disoriented
Making the elders wonder
Whether I was bummed out from the start,
Were under no obligation,
Swore no vows, no promises broken
And to this day
Under my somewhat acclaim
Declaring to friends
That you knew me when I was eighteen.
I now wish you were Anais Nin.
(Although we did down a quart of vodka
Along Northwestern's lake shore drive.)
It takes no heightened event
The ecstatic visitations
Of death, sleep or wine
To bring you to my mind.
Always like a sudden breeze
Briefly passing but clear outlined
Inadvertent and unexpected
Although other women deserved better
It is only your face that I see
Interrupting the flow of time.

9.
"A wretch like me"
Sounds awfully flat

Like striking out before your at-bat
It's like closeting in a bunker
In a field of green
Where much is still to be seen
And certainly more to be asked.
Not to be cursed
But to be cured
Is our task.
Waxing strains of bountiful verse
Expressive energy that does not wane
Accumulations of thought
In a circle of lights
Heading from yesterday to tomorrow
And even better days.

What a revolution that would take
A change of gait in the manners of speech
And easy confidence within our reach
Feelings of welcome and innocence bright
Words not to be checked before they take flight
Checked and quartered by faltering fright.
Words spoken to congenial minds
No need to hold back
The expansion of discourse
Flowing like flowers in a field
A winning habit, a suppleness of choice
Bathed in a circumambient warmth.
A feast of food on a table of cheer
We should do no less for our lifetime here.

10.
He dropped the reins insolently by the shore
Picking his teeth with a haughty sneer.
Through the riot of pounding waves
I appealed to all who might be near
That I didn't even know the lout
But who can make the sea understand
She takes all things with equal hand.

Wallet Poems V

1. Foul and Fair
Weather vanes will turn
And roulettes will spin
Marking a sudden shift
From pained loss to rollicking win.
Or a lack of rain
Can wither bonny into bane.
Handy-dandy is an easy slip
Warning how quickly pulp becomes rind.
Where does that leave the directions of mind?

"Foul-weather friend" is a coinage
Of recent commendable use
Some would call it a friend in need
But Job's comforters is a better feed
Thus given over to some abuse
Like Shakespeare's flowers that rankle
Especially here perversity abounds
Somewhat suspicious those mounds
Of care spewing like lava
But are dollops of syrup instead
Such sweets can choke the flowers,
Attack the pith, are worse than weeds
Where dismay is on demand.
Loving you to death as your organs fail
The foul-weather friend
Smudges his own motive
Which he cannot wipe clean
He enjoys too much his role in the scene.

A "fair-weather friend"
Was a term of abuse
Now we find it more helpful in use.
A fair-weather friend
Will not cringe, be staggered

When you are put on parade;
He will not swallow, and swallow hard
At the drum rolls of success,
Those horses that harnessed
High-step your carriage
Through paths of confetti.
Let the weather turn
And the balls spin
A fair-weather friend plays black or red
Through thick or thin
Because his motives are clear
He responds with his own cheer
There is no grimy edge
That makes him turn halter
No fear that drives him to falter.

The weather vane turns
The roulette ball spins
There are many spots for chances
But I will make more choices
To side with those
Who delight in my wins
Than those who beggar my losses.

Bloc Notes

1.
Wallet Poems has run its course
Fulfilling its purpose as all genres must
Not by dearth but by superflux
Bringing about its own demise:
It has simply surpassed itself.
Just look at the example above,
Or "Dirge for Mary" and "Words, words, words."
Gone is the bouncing wit
The singularity of motive
That made a wallet poem fit
I must bury them justified.
And submit a new turn of verse
Without which no poet can thrive.

2.
In God's universe of compensation
No person should hold all the cards
So how then explain Sam Shepherd?
Handsome, skilled, creative and profound
An actor, with Jessica Lange besides.
The hare who does not stop to snooze
(What need more to prove proverbs banal).
There is only one way to effect a trade-off:
Imagine he invested with Bernie Madoff.

3.
The Catholic girl from Ohio
Had little resource for taking her fill
That is why she turned to Spanish—
Kiting the advantages of another tongue—
But the wings of rebellion were already in flight,
Besides the teacher was cute.
So, while the world teemed to the stadium
To watch the Buckeyes pummel its foes

Led by Woody who controlled the state
She retired to the library
Sharpening her credentials for Phi Bete
But feeling a bit of the odd duck
No cheerleader, no sorority function
She even married a Jewish boy
One certain coup de grace in Ohio
Although the first shot may have been fired
When she tried sex-talk with her mother—in Ohio?
So she and her husband moved to California
Where people are free to pursue their ways—
The real reason California is golden.
Honoring tradition she keeps Jewish holidays
With even a mazuzah on the door
While all their sons go to Catholic schools
What better way to buckle the latch
Than such readiness to mix and match?

4.
Some say rhyme is no longer *du jour*
I add tout quick several arguments
That serve to rebut such thinning concerns.
Rhyme is like a gift, unsolicited
With no strong-arm tactics to force the sense;
But when it comes uninvited
It should not be abandoned, a door-step child
Marked "return to sender"
Spurned, unopened, unexplored
To close down borders is clearly a mistake.
Let gifts pass unimpeded, unimplored.
Pablo Casals is also called in defense—
The foremost cellist of his time—
Who threw up his hands at his American pupils
Who must all have come from the Plains
Where all the talk must be small
Leitotes the regional plant
(But must the music also be flat?)
Fear of stepping on toes

Play it safe by hugging the ground.
Then no gods will punish the chorus
Already divested, plucked clean
Enough to make Casals scream
End with a flourish, go out in style
Assert with freedom a god-given right.
Be bold, be brazen, *abondanza* fulfilled
Let poetry declaim
And when it does let it chant in rhyme.

5.
Among the several phrases I deplore
"Wordsmith" is culturally pretentious
While "parameters" is bureaucratic gore;
"Sucks" and "butt" are simply vulgar
And have never crossed my door.
But phrases that give me the shivers
Are those like "force of nature,"
As if a simple little aneurysm
A break in the rubber on the road
Could not bring this giant to the floor
Or have his car enter the décor
Leaving the consequences so dire
That one would almost beg to expire.
Then the phrase you heard grown-ups speak,
"The love of my life,"
The one you were aching to recite.
When I hear it I want to hide
Knowing that some fortune will be fleeced
And love sheared, with life not long in line.

But this is Nature's plan
By its own dread uses
Challenging our linguistic abuses
Exposing by its lessons stern
That language comprises acts
And is not immune to facts.

Spoiler Speech

To learn where spoiler speech comes from
Takes some digging about.
It's not like spoilage or breakage
Which take the back door out—
Normal costs of doing business.

Spoiler speech is a stricken speech
And goes a long ways back
Like Achilles refusing to bend
But instead takes to his tent;
Which ultimately cost his friend.
One finds it in French duelists
An anger that holds
And allows no retreat.
Which explains why
Anger ranks so high
In the annals of vice
It is so irretrievable, irreversible
Like a gun going off
From which there is no relent.

We can go back on time's arrow,
Collect the pieces,
With softer words make a new start.
But anger affords no such release
Its weapon is spoiler speech;
Spoiler speech that has its center
In the foundries of the heart,
Where over-taxed minions,
Their jump suits soaked with sludge,
Discharge atoms of anger
That are obscurely terse
With many an unknown curse
Doing work that is deadly and dire
Cutting slabs of steel that they must edge,

Leaving fingers stumpy, knees gimpy
And toes all messed up.
It must be from such kind of place
That spoiler speech derives
How else explain those sudden blasts
With which it arrives?

It's like when we slam the door
In a particularly definitive way
Punctuating the vows we made
In a very theatrical display:
"You will never see me again,"
Or, "That's the last time we meet."
Oh ever, forever, never
So long its language runs
It's not as if we came with a bag of guns
Ready to decimate a schoolroom
A venture of long devising;
This was a sudden ambush
From which a working pause
A pinch of winning wit and ease
Would have brought some relief
Or commuted the length of years
From the heavy sentence it bears.

But under the blinding foundry fury
We decide but not by decision
To break with a gradual world
To launch out into the void
And yield to finalities not of our mold
Or habit, some bizarre eruptions
In the ligatures of time.
But after those doors closed forever
We learn how fragile is the core
We do not encounter paths that flourish
Redemptions washing us clean
Or enjoyment of things that nourish
But instead long-lying fields of ice

As far as the eye can see
And steps can wander
The consequences of spoiler speech
And interminableness that comes to be
Perverse companion to finality.

A New Beginning
(Homage for Robin: "All good things connect")

Don't load the artist with humanitarian creeds
Or come at him with legendary complaints
About social conscience, which, for all we know
He might well support, even globalization
Has stirred his ire, but not his art:
They will always be with us.
As well they should be in their changing forms
That continue to draw out human protest
Whatever the conditions or changes in norms.
From within and without we have occasion for rage
Like hungry animals pacing in a cage.
But a new Creation can change all that
Bringing about a generation of folk
Who gather about the works
Made of joy, silence, and water turned to stone.

The only alliance the artist can accept
Is that of his own choosing.
In murderous times his silence is blest
When tanks are crushing Prague
Or any European city
Who can listen to Donizetti?
The vigil of silence is the way of honor
Nor are tears to be disowned
Though not for the showing
They are about their ready business
Of slowly accumulating in ways unknown
Triumphs of music, words and stone.
Such works fostered in stealth
Have their own dispensations
Waiting their moments
When silence has worked its task
And a different soldiery is afoot
Coming from unvisited, unexpected mazes

Representing again the joy of those
Who found their peace and their places
Among those who held their stations.

There are years of public convergence,
Great gatherings as in 1921
But the real miracle occurred
When war had flattened expectations
And those who understood the situation,
Its arching forms and real pressures
Were summoning through tunnels of mind
Their soon unveiled treasures
That were there all the while
Simply awaiting their time
When they could come forward
Announcing themselves in the fullness of rhyme.

Sullen trudging of soldier's boots
Cannot snuff out by curfew or crime
The hidden forms shaped by design
And when the captors are beaten home
They can emerge from darkened caverns
And uncover their splendors of light,
New creations of being
Transformed beyond the grasps of might.

And the people, the people
After forty months or forty years of drought
Burst forth from their collapsed timbers
To sing and dance to the pleasure
Of cadenced numbers
New songs of a second Creation.
The first was obviously a dud.
Speaking of unfair burdens
And calamitous calculations,
In the first days the Spirit did wonders
But what could it have been thinking
Forbidding Eve, so eager to know,

To taste of the tree where knowing can grow.
It might as well have waved a red flag
Asperger syndrome started then
Imagine allowing that sleek serpent
To close and whisper in her ear.
What could be expected but a fallen race
From talent suppressed and passions ignored?
But after that grave mishap
Bringing on chaos and destruction
In a long twisting downward spiral
As if there were no end
But new pains coming upon pain
Beneath the bottoms already sustained,
After such familiarity with crime and desolation
There can only come renewal.
People regained their breath again,
A new mentality of lessened demands
Of living within means and with social graces
And intellectual justice the standard that prevailed
No need to march arm-in-arm
To unison's beat
Each went their separate streets
But graced with recognitions of others' worth
No longer thought that in their principles
They were the only ones always right
Or pounding tables with heavy fists.
The solemnity of costs had ended all that
But willing to let justness abound.
The lessons learned from this new tact
Is that Creations are best after the fact.

Society and art came together at last
The vision of one joined with joy of the other
No one needed to call anyone brother
Nor felt some sin to atone
But rather to praise and defer
To the excellence of those
Whose strategies of retreat did not lie fallow

But molded the waters that flowed
Into objects of solace, comfort and joy.

The people, following some directing purpose,
Gathered at the fountains
Where the first miracles were born
When water running like time itself
Conferred motion on rough-hewn stone
And unmoving horses then seemed to gallop
Raise up and neigh
While streams pitched like fallen rain
With glistening colors down tangled manes
The people now embraced a public art
A spectacle commingling mind and heart.
Metamorphoses of being
Transformations of form
Came together as humankind wagered a new start.

Early and Late: The Hazards of the Ways

Tsi Giovan claimed it for the Italians
Big Mike rose to his full height
And insisted it was the Irish
Who laid the great railroad track
Pounding the table with accented fist.
Could one really dissent
From such embodied voice?
Like Chaucer's monk
They eliminated any workings of choice.
They were men of the middle passage
Connecting the old with the new country
Who labored the ways for others to travel;
They were the courageous, the uprooted,
Who also bent deep in the mines
To bring up the coal, that fired the steam
That sent the giant machines
Like black birds of thunder screeching loud
Crisscrossing America's fruitful plains
Joining us all in the new Age of Steel,
Railroads comprising the central appeal.

Of this we kids had no conception
But enjoyed its means nonetheless
During WWII we scoured the tracks
Hunting for scraps of iron
That brought ten cents a pound
But always on the look-out
For Straity the railroad dick
Who could come swooping down
Waving his pistol
Carousing some shots
That put us on the run,
All the while laughing and taunting
Leaving him back a sure half-mile.
The railroad tracks were our roadways

To get where we were going
Even hitching onto a slowing freight,
A wind-swept joy ride
Stretching with one hand outright
And one leg spread-eagle in flight.

To get to a spit of land
With a gradual fall-off into the river
We had to cross over a single-track trestle
If surprised by an oncoming monster
We had to jump for cover
Either to land's edge
Or else reach the ledge
Of a rampart supporting the bridge
And cling to the shaking cable
That ran its length
Hugging tightly for victory
And a final way back,
And we not even ten
Well before the war's end.
We may have sensed but did not know
That death was all around us.
This world was our natural playground
With its own hard rules
Depression-bred, wartime-bound
The costly cut of human price.

Early and late
In the beginning and near its ending date
The railroads were chosen
As fitting emblems of our times
To convey our memories, our men—
A long-winding entourage of mourning—
From the great Lincoln
To the man who should have been.
It was the railroads that carried them
Through the lands of their natural constituency
Lincoln back to Springfield

And Bobby to the Arlington soil.
The people came together
Forming an unending honor guard
Unbroken strings along the iron rails
They pressed and massed tightly
Retinues of peopled swag
Pushing along the mounds of slag
Trying to keep pace
Or stay the trains in their carriage.

Thus children and grown men came together
As part of the same epochal reign
The young so happily unaware
But the old, they came to bear
The choices they were constrained to make
Their own fates obscurely present
Closing like manacles to where they were bound
They felt the tightened circles of iron
The circumscription of their ends.
Bobby saw them in the crowded mikes
Pointed like pistols to his head,
Their sacrifices were continuous, enduring
But without commensurate gain
Lincoln's work was done
But then undone by Jim Crow
Requiring another hundred years
Another tumultuous 'Sixties
That brought down Bobby
And continued the war
For five more years and 50,000 dead,
And the only President who resigned in disgrace
Lincoln's successor—another Johnson—
Almost met a similar end.
Thus decline like rot took hold
Auto makers with their freeways routed the trains
Simpler ways of coming together were derailed
And public service faltered and then failed
There was no way to cover the loss.

The auto created its own mischance
Breathing in its standing waste
Even increasing lanes brings no relief
By such means are we entangled
That all labor mars what it does.
There's no way out; we play a losing game,
Our own devices are countervailing gains.

But another lesson might here be derived
That men of greatness held in mind
When latching their belts
(With Dante, Shakespeare and Aeschylus)
That mortality attends each chosen way
That permanence and power cannot coincide
And that the means of our living
Is the trough of our demise.

Ricardo Quinones is a scholar-critic, professor emeritus of Claremont McKenna College. He is the author of such prize-winning volumes as *The Changes of Cain: Violence and the Lost Brother in Cain-Abel Literature* (1991) and *Dualisms: The Agons of the Modern World* (2007), which was followed by *Erasmus and Voltaire: Why They Still Matter* (2010) and *North/South: The Great European Divide* (2016).